Heart

Heart

Wisdom Awakening

Nanna Aida Svendsen

Copyright Nanna Svendsen © 2015
First published in 2015 by Pleasant House Ltd
BM Box 6100, Monomark House
27 Old Gloucester Street, London WC1N 3XX
www.pleasanthouse.com

Distributed by Gardners Books, 1 Whittle Drive, Eastbourne,
East Sussex, BN23 6QH

The right of Nanna Svendsen to be identified as the author of the work has been asserted herein in accordance with the Copyright, Designs and Patents Act 1988.

All rights reserved. This book is sold subject to the condition that it shall not, by way of trade or otherwise, be lent, resold, hired out or otherwise circulated without the publisher's prior consent in any form of binding or cover other than that in which it is published and without a similar condition including this condition being imposed on the subsequent purchaser.

British Library Cataloguing in Publication Data
A catalogue record for this book is available from the British Library.

ISBN 978-0-9555080-1-1

Typeset by Amolibros, Milverton, Somerset
www.amolibros.com
This book production has been managed by Amolibros
Printed and bound by T J International Ltd, Padstow, Cornwall, UK

Contents

What Others Have Said	viii
Dedication	ix
Acknowledgements	x
About Nanna Aida Svendsen	xi

Prologue — 1

Make A Sanctuary: Moments Of Stillness	2

Summer: Tending Inner Seas — 5

Momentous Days: A Threshold Between Worlds	6
In Transition: Letting Psyche Do Her Work	9
Traveller Trance: Seven Days	11
Meanwhile The Swan: Needing Rest	13
Falling Down: Time For Descent	15
A Message From The Mermaids: Tend Your Inner Sea	17
Glimmer Of Temptation: Hooked By A Core Wound	19
Not Enough: The Fear We Might Not Cut It	22
Wild Pansies: Finding Heart's Ease	25
Morning Reflection: Being Preoccupied	26
Boredom: A Message From The Heart	28
Frail Light: Regret	30
Not An Act Of Will: You Can't Force A Feeling	32
Hidden Gems: Places Where We Falter	34
Although You Are Gone: When Someone Dies…	38
A Quiet Rebel-Lion: Called To Awaken	42

Autumn: Letting Go — 45

Lying Fallow: Resting, Recovering, Readying	46
Silence: Inner Compass	48
Silent Pulse: A Place Of Resonance	50
Longing: A Rendering Of Existence	52
Huddled In The Rain: A Time To Wait	55
Could It Be The Moon? Called To Evolve	57
Fall Reflections: Fragile Beauty	60
Loss: A Sense Of Sorrow	61
Moon Above A Fir Tree: Beauty In Heartbreak	64
The Seal: A Gift Of Communion	66
A Place Of Grace: Falling In Love With The World	68

Winter: Cherishing The Heart — 71

Winter In Andalusia: A Tender Luminescence	72
Child Within: Essence Of Who We Are	74
Footprints On The Beach: Interweaving With Life	78
What Belongs: Discarding Old Forms	80
When Time Is Ripe: Waiting For Wisdom To Arise	82
Subdued Light: Holding Still	85
Tangling With The Muse: Called By The Creative	87
Holding The Space: Being Attentive To A Process	89
Snow Apples: Welcoming The Heart	92
Two Deer: Tender Relating	95
Cupid's Arrow – A Poem Of Love	98
An Umbrella Of Compassion: Cherishing The Heart	101
The Heart Awakens: Being Response-Able	104
The Heart Opens: The Gift Of Vulnerability	106
Tears Come Easily: Susceptible To Life	108
Listen: When Everything Feels Too Much	110
How To Be Gentle: The Soft Voice Of The Soul	112
Midwinter Still: Pregnant With Possibility	114
Mending Nets: Receiving Deeper Wisdom	117

Thinking Of Snowdrops: Dropping Ambition	119
A Small Swan Tear: Grief And Relief	121

Spring: Sourced In Inner Wisdom   *127*

Betwixt And Between: Waiting For Hidden Life To Take Form	128
Not As It Seems: A Deeper Truth	130
Screens Of Smoke: The Mind Starts	132
You Can't Get There From Here: A Matter Of Surrender	135
A Butterfly Waits: Trusting The Process	138
Mouse Ears: Listening For Inspiration	142
Beckoned By The Moon: Called By The Feminine	144
Like A Peony: Remembering The Grace Of The Feminine	147
Do Not Forget: Tend Yourself, Tend The Earth	150
Tangles Of Wild Flowers: Energy Is A Form Of Intelligence	152
Cows: Freedom, Spontaneity And Delight	155
School Children: Waiting To Blossom	157
The Flower That You Are: All You Want To Do	160
Cherry Blossoms: Darkness And Light	162
The Garden Of Your Love: For A Wedding	164

Epilogue   *167*

Wisdom Awakening: A Poem In Three Parts	168
Wisdom Awakening One: Being Called Home	168
Wisdom Awakening Two: Connecting With Your Soul Child	169
Wisdom Awakening Three: A Sacred Union	171

What Others Have Said About Nanna's Work

"Nanna's words heal. Her poetry is balm for the soul, a language of the heart that returns us to what matters most in life."

Cheryl Richardson best selling American author, life coach, presenter and broadcaster.

"What can I say? Your poems help us reach inside ourselves to our essence. They help us remember who we are. They are fierce with tenderness, truth and love."

Christiane Northrup MD. Noted American visionary, writer, speaker and television personality.

"Svendsen has really thought about the essence of things, the emotional machinery of living, and there is something really appealing about her crisp and almost visionary observations. She shifts the shadows to show light, shifts the light to show shadows. There is no cleverness, no word-magic, just the offering of some cold and warming eternal truths."

Peter Thabit Jones editor Seventh Quarry Poetry Magazine, Wales

"Nanna's poems are full of the charm of an innocent child, the passion of a feminine heart and the wisdom of the deepest soul. I am always opened and transformed by them."

Eva Sanner Swedish author and therapist

For my beloved Carl,
My little family in Spain,
The rest of my family,
And my friends.

      Love you
      Always...

           Nanna Aida Svendsen

Acknowledgements

Special thanks go to Punit Krejsgaard for living the work with me and for her exquisite editorial support.

To Jane Tatam of Amolibros for turning my raw manuscript into a book for the second time! It would not have been nearly as joyful a process or so beautiful a book without her help. I am so grateful.

And to my beloved Carl Lindstrom for his ongoing love, inspiration and support. He truly is the companion of my heart.

About Nanna Aida Svendsen

Nanna Aida Svendsen is an explorer and mapmaker of the inner realms, writer and poet. Her passion is linking consciousness with the heart and feeling into the emergent, naming where consciousness wants to evolve, and what might be getting in the way. Something she likes to do on her blog, in her writing, in poetry readings, and in the soul time groups she runs.

She has said of her work, "It has long been the job of artists and poets to feel into the present and give language to what is. Give language to feeling and insight that others too might recognize aspects of themselves and find their lives reflected in the words. It is also the job of the poet to inhabit the unfolding edge of the unknown, and to write about that, as well as write about what is emerging." Though rigourous at times this is work that Nanna loves.

Born in England, she grew up in Denmark, lived in the US for many years and currently makes her home with her husband in Sweden.

Her book *Of Water Liles and Warm Hearts* has been translated into Swedish by Eva Sanner, and many of the poems in this book have been translated in to Swedish by Asa Leander. Please go to the website www.pleasanthouse.com for more information about both the English and Swedish versions as well as her fairy tale *Freya and the Magic Cloak*.

For her blog and more of her poems and reflections, please go to www.soultimereflections.com.

Prologue

Make A Sanctuary: Moments Of Stillness

Know what you do
With your life really matters.
The future of humanity
May depend on it.

Find the core of your compassion
For yourself and others
And let the grace of love and kindliness
Be your guide.

Follow the calling of your heart.
This might sound simple, it isn't.
To walk a loving path,
The one that is yours alone to walk,
Will cost you everything
That isn't genuine
And in return
It will give you everything
That is…

Make a sanctuary of your life.
In moments of stillness
Stop, listen, reflect,
And help make the world a safe haven
For hearts and souls alike.

The future of humanity
May depend on it.

The above came in moments of stillness. In a way it is the essence of the work. So I would like to share it here with you as a prelude to the book, which is after all about making a sanctuary of heart-full loving kindness for ourselves, and so perhaps for others and for the world.

Summer: Tending Inner Seas

Momentous Days: A Threshold Between Worlds

These are momentous days
We are standing
On a threshold between worlds.

Old ways that diminish
Who we are,
May be rubbing up
Against the emergent
And perhaps giving way

To the evolving
To the unknown and hopefully
Though not necessarily
The encouraging.

These are momentous days.
The world as we know it
Is wavering on the edge
Of disaster.

What will we do?

Will we cling
To the outmoded
In our lives?
Hold on to the familiar
Even if
It no longer is sustaining?

Will angst clutch our hearts?
Hold us hostage
To ways of being
A deeper part of us knows
We do not want?

Will we teeter on the edge
Of love and fear?

Or, with trembling grace
And trepidation
Might we choose the original?
The one life
That is ours alone to inhabit?

Might we connect
With the essential,
The perennial,
The arising?
Find and follow
The path with heart?

Might we surrender
To what we truly deeply love
To what really matters most?

Might we find and be the forms
That nourish and support
Humanity?

Might we start
Inhabiting the Coeur-age?

Summer solstice today. A day tradition has it, here in the north, of dancing round the maypole, or lighting bonfires, singing songs and celebrating the height of the light. We are in the season of white nights. At this time of year midnight appears as a grey dusk with the sun having only just set to the west before almost immediately rising to the east. By August 1st, halfway between solstice and autumn equinox, the nights will already have drawn in with darkness falling around nine p.m.

But for now the light is with us. Wonderful as this may be, it is also demanding. All that light can have a relentless quality from which at times there seems nowhere to retreat to or to hide. And light is also able to illuminate issues we have kept hidden from ourselves, one another, or as a culture. Particularly perhaps at a time in which so many of us find ourselves poised on the threshold between what we once knew and trusted, that no longer can support us, and the call of the unfamiliar, yet hopefully more sustaining. A threshold we may not have volunteered for.

It is challenging to be on the brink. There may be grief or a sense of betrayal in the loss of the old that needs to be recognized and given its due before we can find the wherewithal to continue. The initial steps may be tentative. Is where we are headed really where we want to go?

In Transition: Letting Psyche Do Her Work

The intense summer heat
Continues.
The signets
Have grown big.
And I am on the threshold
Of journey.
Family is calling.

Though there is sadness
To the leaving,
There is also joy to the going.

Psyche meanwhile
Is keeping busy with her plans
And preparations.
She is building energetic bridges
To carry me across
A wild and tossing sea.

Platforms of remembered scenes
Intertwined with prospects
Are being structured
To support me.
I am already partly there.

Quietly insistent
Psyche does her work.
All I can do is let her

And trust love's calling
Now taking me away
Also to bring me home.

Like so many of us in summer I am going on my holidays. Hopes, ideas and plans are starting to form. Yes. I am looking forward. There is a soft excitement. There is also trepidation. Fears and resistances are emerging. Is what is intended truly supportive of what a deeper part of me knows, longs for and loves? Do I really want to go? Thank-fully yes.

Every journey is, in a sense, a little dying. The way things are is ending. A venturing out into another land is beginning, figuratively, if not literally. Even if circumstances may appear the same upon returning, there is no guarantee that I will be the same as when I left.

Traveller Trance: Seven Days

I have been on a journey.
Seven foreign cities
In seven days.

The traveller trance has had me.
Psyche has been busy
Exploring, experiencing
Navigating and adapting
To the unfamiliar.

Attention has been focused
On the outer.

Now coming home
I find that trance
Difficult to shift.

It takes time to return,
To integrate all those impressions,
Rest, reconfigure and reconnect
With the inner, the writer
And the poet.
It takes time for reflection.

I have been on a journey.
Seven foreign cities
In seven days.
It is taking it seems
At least seven days
To recover.

I wrote the poem above because I wanted to say something about not only the process of being away, but also about the process of returning. I have found many a time that the journey home to myself in the wake of a voyage is often as demanding as the voyage itself. In some ways it is where the real learning, and integration of insight takes place.

As far as I can tell this is an aspect of travel rarely spoken of or acknowledged. One we rarely give ourselves or each other time for. Yet it may well apply to any kind of change in our lives. It is after the event itself that recovery, and all that this implies, begins.

Meanwhile The Swan: Needing Rest

meanwhile the swan
echoing the mood of the moment
has lumbered up on land
and is resting on the lawn

not for her now to swim
against the current
rather she is waiting
for rough waters to still

for time to be ripe
for movement
in accord
with body heart and soul

Tired today. I am in need of rest, which I have come to think of as time for:

Retreat, reflection and regeneration,
   Emotional awareness and release,
      Stillness and being in the silence,
         Tuning in to the essence of myself and existence

Choosing to stop what we are doing and rest is a radical yet essential act of self-cherishing. It may not only help us regenerate to the core, it may also challenge us to question what is happening to us, thanks to all our doing, and to ponder if this is truly what we want.

Summer as it happens is a perfect time to rest if we will but take the time. The old school year is over, on so many levels. The holidays can be a time of recognizing where we are, relinquishing the grip of what is ending and opening ourselves to the emergent. A time for letting ourselves mature emotionally, like fruit on the bough until we are ready to let go and fall into the next stage of life's journey.

Falling Down: Time For Descent

We try so hard
To stay up
To keep from falling down
Yet there is a falling
Into ourselves
That is of the essence.

There is a tumbling into the heart
That means we must open
To our beauty and our pain.

Without a willingness
To surrender
To a flow of feelings,
Receive them with compassion,
We may never come to know
That sweet sense
Of oneness with ourselves,
That simple bliss
In being
Beneath all our distress.

Without a willingness
To surrender
And turn attention
To the quiet
That underlies the turmoil
Of the mind
We may never come to know
That sweet sense
Of oneness

With existence,
That sweet sense
Of love and trust and flow.

We try so hard to stay up
Yet there is a falling down
That is of the essence.

We seem to be living in a culture that asks that we be up most of the time, on the go, achieving or producing things. We even insist, at least in our cities, on the bright light of day, or as near as, 24/7. We claim not to like darkness and down time. We leave little space for those necessary times of withdrawal and retreat into ourselves that help us rest, regenerate, reintegrate and refine aspects of ourselves, in need of attention. We have little tolerance for descent.

We seem to ignore the fact that down time is part of any creative or healing journey. Grieving is the way we complete things emotionally. Often we don't offer or take time for this either. We consider descent a disease, and do all that we can to avoid it, and certainly we do not want to admit to it. Yet sometimes it seems we must fall off the track, which may in part have been laid out for us by others, so as to find and follow our own true path.

A Message From The Mermaids: Tend Your Inner Sea

Down on the dock with the morning
The silver sea reflective, still.
Liquid gold spangles trail
Across the water
Like shining locks of some mermaid
Drifting with the deep.

With a sudden ruffle of small waves
I thought I heard the mermaid sing.

The sea…the sea is dying. Its riches ravaged.
It is being plundered and polluted.
Save the sea!
Save the sea
If you will save yourselves.

I felt myself reach out.
How? How? Shall I save the sea?

With a golden shimmer of the water
A soft whisper of the waves
She replied:

Tend your inner sea.
Take time to mend your heart
And cherish what you love.

Her words struck a chord.
As I sat dreaming on the dock.
Tend my inner sea

Mend my heart
And cherish what I love.

The golden spangles
Trailed across the deep
Have gone now.
Not so the spangles of my heart.
They're still here.
Quietly, softly shining
Waiting to show me the way
If I choose to find and follow it.

A friend came to visit from New York. She was passionate about saving the oceans, and about mermaids. She said every culture has a mermaid myth, and that in every myth the thing that does the mermaid in is not getting enough down time to herself in the deep.

This is indeed a sorrow of our time, losing our connection to the needs and wisdom of the inner mermaid, symbol of the inner feminine, the intuitive, receptive, reflective, relational side of us. So many of us are stressed, depleted and burned out, for want of time in the deep with the feminine. It also occurred to me that there may be a link between the way we relate to and care for our inner sea, our emotions and feelings, and the way we relate to and care for the sea, and indeed the earth itself.

Glimmer Of Temptation: Hooked By A Core Wound

Here it comes again
The thought, the fear
The tension, the idea

That in order to stay safe
And be attractive
I should be different.

That primal ravage
The fatal
Should
Is tugging at my heart.

I can feel the hook going in.

To try and make you love me
By foregoing
My true feelings and my needs,
And being defined by yours.

Oh that shimmering allurement
Of your love
Seems so enticing…
I can feel myself reeled in.
How can I refuse?
How avoid the shame if I say no?

What will I do?

Will I stay hooked on your line
And struggle yet again
To be other than I am?
Will I tear myself apart?

Or will I recognize the damage
And the danger
For what it is?

Allow the sorrow
I am not all
You or I think
I should be

And finally, finally
Surrender to my essence.
My life as it unfolds,
And let myself off the hook?

There seems to be something about this time in which many of us are being hooked by our core wound. The place in us, in which we closed our hearts to something essential, in order to please or appease and stay safe. This may seem like nothing. But this is serious.

For this go-round, at least for some, it is a wound sustained from an emotional and cultural inheritance built on gaining power by using shame and blame. A cultural inheritance, transferred from one emotionally wounded to another, rendering a world devoid of empathy and heart. A world that requires we do what we should, and become a function that fits its form and serves its purpose, no matter the cost to aliveness, integrity, and well being.

For this go-round the wound has been re-awoken by being shamed, or betrayed in the sharing of our gifts, by those we thought we could depend on. There is something particularly ravaging about this.

Hurt in our heart place, it displays its pain in anger, sorrow, fear, or confusion. It may go numb or writhe in silent agony. The body, repository of all this, shows it symptoms: migraines, indigestion, skin eruptions, allergies, dizziness, back-aches and more, have been flaring for many.

It can take a fair bit of awareness and work to shrug off the hold of a wound, extricate ourselves from its hook, and return to a sense of wholeness, and integrity, inside.

In my experience the hook cannot be removed until it has been accurately named and described. Empathy as well as insight from the wise part of us, or the wise part of someone else, will be needed. And of course the lesson, as always is not to continue betraying ourselves, or others, in any fundamental way.

Inventor and philosopher Buckminster Fuller used to say we are living at a time in which humanity is up for its final exam to determine whether we have the integrity, individually and collectively, to continue as a species in the universe. Perhaps he was right? Perhaps the integral work of whole making on the inner, becoming more sound of heart, and less defined by our wound, is of crucial importance now?

Not Enough: The Fear We Might Not Cut It

There is a fear
That who we are
Is not enough.
That we must be more,
Better, different,
Thinner, fatter,
Stronger, younger, older,
More expressive
Or more silent.
Able to do something,
Anything,
Other than be who
And how we are,
To stay safe.
To be someone
Worthy of support
Recognition
Payment
Love.
There is so much invested
In our doing what
We do not want to do
To survive.
So much identity and dependency
Bound up in ideas
Of what it takes
To make it
They have become a cultural habit.

It takes intention
Delicate, determined excavation
To break the hold
Of the addiction
And unearth the essential
Sense of self
That sacred originality
Interlaced with life
At our core.

It takes the willingness
To be
Extraordinary and ordinary.
To do what feels good
And follow the moment.
Even then
There can be anxiety
That being present
With our deeper selves
Inhabiting our souls calling
And living what we love,
Will not be enough
To keep us safe.

Meanwhile the world
Is going crazy
For want of presence,
Safety and love.

Not the kind of safety
To which we are accustomed,
Not the kind of love.
The kind that costs us

Who we are.
Which is no safety, or love, at all.
But the kind
That invites us to be
Nothing more, nothing less,
Than our deepest, truest, beloved selves,
Evolving in communion with existence
As it unfolds.

The kind of safety,
At least inside ourselves,
That allows us to know
Who we are is essential,
Is the gift,
And enough.

The swan came to the dock again today. Right up close where I was sitting, she nibbled at the reeds flanked by flurry of sparkles. Sometimes simply being with the swan is enough. This feels vital. I wrote this poem in response to a friend who told me she did not have the energy, or the desire, for all she felt she had to do, and did not feel she was enough.

Wild Pansies: Finding Heart's Ease

Wild pansies growing
In the verge
Along the lane

Their blue and yellow faces
Bathing in bright sunlight,
As cozy, midst tall grasses,
They are sheltered
From too much breeze.

Their hearts seem at ease
Nothing now disturbs
Their fragile
Beauty.

I love seeing wild pansies growing along the lane and in the garden. Their bright little faces bring a spread of color, and speak of delighting in summer sunshine. Heartsease seems a good name. The simple pleasure in finding them does ease my heart and reminds me that nothing more is needed now other than delighting in their company.

Morning Reflection: Being Preoccupied

Nature doesn't speak
to me today.

A swan nibbles
with desultory bites
and tugs, at the reeds,
barely moves
a still and silent sea.

I am preoccupied
Working something out.

The swan
by the dock
has no meaning now.

I was looking forward to having a cup of tea on the dock. However when I arrived there with the tea tray I discovered I had forgotten to bring the tea!

What was going on? In a culture obsessed with aging, and any sign of memory loss, I understandably was concerned. I checked the usual suspects that can impact memory: worry, stress, depression, sleeplessness, being overwhelmed, in a mood, or taken by an emotional wound, but none were troubling me that day.

Suddenly I got it. When I had left the kitchen I had been entirely preoccupied with an idea for the writing. Creative work had me. I was present to that, trying to work something out, rather than being present to the bringing of the tea.

I have noticed before, that like some absent-minded professor when engrossed in a topic, attention for and memory off other things might elude me for a while. There is certain beauty to this. It can allow me to stay present with whatever it is I have given myself over to and maintain awareness with that. In a certain sense it is the opposite of multi-tasking, it is being fully present to just one person or idea.

Not only this, I have found, when deeply preoccupied, or present to something, holding the space for it if you will, it is not always so easy to change my mind from one occupation to another. The swan down by the dock did indeed have little meaning that day. However, the process of being preoccupied, the impact of that, surely did.

Boredom: A Message From The Heart

Yearning for a match
between
what I am doing
and what I long to be doing.

Some deeper need
not being met.
Some realization
not as yet discovered.

Some creative impulse
not yet ready
or not allowed to unfold.

Boredom.

Information that what I am doing
or the way I am doing it
has me in thrall
to a moment
or a life
too small for aliveness
to flourish.

I wrote "Boredom" after having found myself stuck in a conversation that was going on and on about something of no interest to me. Somehow I found myself unable, or unwilling, to turn the conversation round, nor was I able to find a kindly way of leaving it. I began describing my feelings to myself and found myself saying: "I am bored now. Bored. Bored. Bored."

Later in the spirit of recognizing feelings as messengers about who and how we are, I felt inspired to explore what that feeling of boredom had been trying to tell me, and came up with the poem.

That profound sense of boredom with the conversation helped inform me that the particular conversation at that time, in that way, did not represent the best use of my energy, my wisdom, my learning or my talents. In some sense soul seemed to be on hold, waiting to return to something furthering.

Of course we may choose at times to stay in boring situations out of a sense of service to some other overriding consideration, empathy for the other person's process perhaps or empathy for our own, a sense of kindness, a willingness not to be too quick to judge?

Indeed boredom can be a part of a creative process. There is a sort of empty no-thing feeling at times as we wait for the well of inspiration to fill and overflow into some more visible form of expression. Boredom need not always be bad. It can at times become a source of inspiration in itself. It is however a form of information worthy of consideration. What is our feeling of boredom trying to tell us? What insight might it wish to convey?

Frail Light: Regret

Regret has been a visitor today
casting its dull hue across the sky
rendering sunlight frail.

Regret with its sorrowing
it's angsting and remorse
it's forgetting
that when one door closes
another sometimes opens.

A lament not so much
for what was done
but more a longing
for what was not.

And who can know the price of that?

Indeed what was chosen
had its wisdom too.
Choices that helped make a life

Regrets once recognized
and understood
that may help
inform a future.

Kindle up a flame bright enough
to illuminate the drear.

Burn right through it
and render the day
shimmering
with allurement yet again.

There can be a sense of shame in association with feelings of regret. Almost as though the culture insists there must be something wrong with us to feel it. And oh, that we must have done something wrong, or have made a mistake otherwise why would we feel like this? Yet to admit regret is to recognise and own what we did, and the choices we have made. It is perhaps a chance to come to appreciate something real about ourselves.

To delve our regretful-ness is to be willing to recognize the reasons we chose as we did. Owning our regret is also a chance to offer ourselves and others forgiveness and compassion. It is an opportunity to make amends, and perhaps make other choices if appropriate? Not as an avoidance of regret but more as a recognition of its wisdom.

To remain stuck in one's regrets and ever defined by them can be a great sorrow. To end one's days with a feeling of regret at having missed one's own life, that something essential remained always unlived, is a sadness too. Far better perhaps to embrace regret, grieve, and recognize its deeper wisdom. To be able to admit regret, delve it, and come to understand the power of its hold, speaks to me of emotional maturity. It speaks of an awakening of the heart.

Not An Act Of Will: You Can't Force A Feeling

A feeling of forgiveness
That surprising sweet relief
Is not an act of will

It is a grace of being
That comes naturally
When the heart

Has had time to reflect
And ripen
In the light of awareness

Like some fruit
On the bough
Maturing in the moonlight
And ripening in the sun

Until it is ready
To drop
From the tree
By itself.

The feeling of forgiveness can be one of palpable relief. It can bring a sense of ease to the soul. Not to be confused with condoning, forgetting, or agreeing to put up with intolerable behavior, rather forgiveness is a sense of being released from anger and resentment. A gift of freedom from being defined entirely by one's pain or emotional wound one might enter into and offer oneself, or another.

For all the power of forgiveness, when it is an accurate description of what actually is, it is not an act of will. If I don't feel forgiving I cannot force the sense of it. One day when working in my journal around an issue of old emotional pain I found myself at the end of the process overwhelmed by a great wave of forgiveness for all concerned. The experience was so strong it inspired this poem about forgiveness. "Not an Act Of Will."

Hidden Gems: Places Where We Falter

We all have places where we falter
Where darkness
Insecurity and discouragement
Drag us down like stones
Into the deep.

We all have times
When a fist of fear or fury,
Old programs or old wounds,
Clenches around the heart
Holding us hostage to a life
We do not want.

We may try to run away
Pretend the fist does not exist
But the faltering remains.

The burden
Of unacknowledged pain
Hiding love and light
Will only be relieved
When we stop.

And willingly or otherwise
Come to recognize the hand
That has held us
All too tightly for so long

Waiting for a time
When we might begin,
With a tender touch of attention

Awareness, and acceptance,
To ease its grip
That the hidden gems of aliveness
And joy
Clasped in its palm might be released.

We all have places where we falter
Where unattended woe
Wears us down.

Don't try to hide
The sorrows of the heart
Sense their presence!

We all have times
When the fist
Clutches us too tightly.
There is no shame in that

And there is beauty to be found
In that hand

When it feels safe to open
Like a flower in the sun
And release
The grief and the grace
Held within it.

I could not resist the photograph "Wing Left Behind" by Jeanne Mayell when I saw it. It seemed to speak to the theme *of Hidden Gems*. For there lingering at the heart of a small flower of many petals, was a sacred jewel, an iridescent insect wing, a gift of grief and of grace, waiting to be revealed as the flower opened.

Jeanne said of this piece, "It took hours of loving attention to find the secret of the tiny chrysanthemum and its even tinier wing. It was a kind of mindfulness exercise – giving some attention and revealing a jewel in something so commonplace."

Yes Jeanne, and doesn't it also take hours of loving attention and mindfulness to find the secrets of the heart? To recognise and soften round our pain, our old wounds, our patterns of survival, and our pleasures? As well as to recognise the beliefs and thoughts we may have formed that do not tally with our deeper knowing and reality – in a certain sense to change our mind and awaken to our sensibilities.

And isn't life also like your photo? As we open to beauty we also must be willing to open to heartache. And when the heart is broken isn't this so often the very thing that opens us to life and to love.

So don't try to hide your sorrow, sense its presence! As my friend Lily likes to say: "Embrace every thread that is woven into the fabric of your being. This includes being fearful, obsessive, lazy, exhausted, moody, as well as mindful, happy, loving," to name but a few of the threads.

It is perhaps the very willingness to receive ourselves, in our pain as well as in our joy, and our willingness to receive others in their pain and their joy, that may help us discover the hidden gems held inside us.

Although You Are Gone: When Someone Dies...

Although you are gone
You are not gone.

You are here
In the reaching field of daisies
Near the house

In the silver flutter
Of the willows growing by the pond

In the pink edged candles on the chestnut,
Its branches bowing
With the breeze.

You are here
In the golden glow across the land

In the white starlight dancing
On the waves
In small fish who like
To jump through the surface
Of the sea.

You are here
In the tiny bird
Singing
Its sacred song

And in the wisdom
Of your words
Still whispered
In my ear.

You are here
In the tender blanket
Love sometimes likes to wrap
Around me

For although you are gone
You are not gone.

Dad died thirteen years ago almost to the day and Mom three years and three months before that. There have been other deaths too of family and friends. This poem was written in memory of them and for anyone who has lost a loved one.

The night I heard Dad had died, I had been on an outing with my honey to one of the Stockholm archipelago's many small islands. Speeding along in a little boat through the dusk, I looked at the sky. It was a dark strangely luminous green-blue and a small waning moon hung high above us accompanied by a solitary star.

I thought of my father then. Felt worried. He had not been well. He was in the hospital. Staring at the star I had the strangest sensation, that it was him, travelling the skies. When I came home there was a message. He had passed on.

The following evening I sat on the dock and searched for that star. And could not find it. Wrapped in a blanket on an old wooden bench by an old wooden table, a lone candle aglow, I tried to write. But could not. Only one thing to do, surrender to the tears and let soul's night descend.

I remember feeling vulnerable. My inner cadence a trembling assailable blue. Grief came in waves. I kept falling back into an old sea of sorrow, as this grief seemed to call forth so many others…Death is a wrench.

I understand why people wear black. Want to carry some sort of sign. Not just because of the grief but also because of the need to show the world that soul has been shocked. Something vulnerable making has happened. Heart is on the surface.

I imagined myself wearing a black band, or carrying a little sign with the words 'black' written on it to be flashed at necessary moments to those who would claim my attention for their own devises, when I could not give it.

A process of inner reorientation was taking place as its wont in the wake of any death or ending of something Yes, the sorrow came in waves. It welled up, sometimes seemingly out of nowhere, and moved through me like those huge slow rollers on the oceans that travel for miles…

Even now one might well within me. Not only grief though, but something more ethereal as well. Some sense of being more susceptible to life, being part of it, with no separation. Not even separate from Mum and Dad. Somehow, somewhere in some strange way, they were and are still here. And certainly the love. The love has gone nowhere. And it never will…

A Quiet Rebel-Lion: Called To Awaken

A quiet rebel-lion is stirring hearts
In the night.

Quiet and in the dark in the sense
The rousing is happening for some
Mostly if not entirely
Within.

A rebel in the sense
Of a growing need
To shrug off old patterns
Of shame and survival
That quell
Aliveness and humanity.
Patterns too small
For the unfolding mystery
Of who we are,

And a lion in the sense,
Of our essence,
In communion with existence,
Are being called
To awaken.

Or you could say
We are being called to have the courage
To wake up to the pain
As well as to the wisdom and grace
Of the inner lion
To our feelings of vulnerability,
Freedom, connectedness
And love.

An opening and a quieting of the mind
A recognising and healing of the heart
May be called for

If we are to enter the Coeur—Age,
Age of the heart of the lion.

Now, as morning sun comes to light the shore, I feel called to awaken. Not only in the sense of greeting a new day but also in another elemental way. Some profound movement towards liberation from behaviours that no longer work for the planet, or for us, seems to be afoot. The evolution of consciousness may be affecting something here, asking us to rouse and bring awareness to what is going on, not only around us, but also inside ourselves. Calling us perhaps to enter the Couer—Age, age of the heart of the lion.

Autumn: Letting Go

Lying Fallow: Resting, Recovering, Readying

after the hecticness of summer
with all that abundant blossoming
thrusting to achieve, bear fruit,
and ripen with the light

after all that intensity
comes the fall
with the advent of darker days
and the need to release
and retreat

lie fallow like the fields
resting, recovering and readying
for the next creative venture
to take form as autumn unfolds.

Dark and grey today. The sky leaden. The sea pewter, a tin drum beaten smooth by the rain. Wet trees hang layered leaves of deepest green with smatterings of gold. Some fall to the sodden earth below, where they lie waiting for the next stage of life's journey to unfold. Into such a morning comes the recognition of needing to lie fallow.

Oh, how little space we leave for fallowness. There seems to be a need to be busy and stimulated all the time. There can be a sense of worthlessness or guilt to the idea of needing to stay silent and gestate. Of having nothing much to say, of not wanting to do anything other than be, of dropping ambition and staying true to the energy of the moment as it reveals itself to us.

So I will tend this liminal moment, as something is integrated, something is relinquished, something is recognised, and some new creative journey, I sense may be waiting round the corner, to show me a hint of the road I might follow to inhabit it.

Silence: Inner Compass

I could not find the voice
that is my own
amidst the cacophony
of sound
that is America to me.

It took the silence of Sweden for that.

The steadfast presence
of those old
round granite rocks
the still reflective sea
the quiet of hidden dells
amidst the pines
dotted with silver birch

the resonance
of the essence and the light
of this place with my soul

to hear the call of the life
that is my own.

The one I have no choice
but to live.

Sheltering from the rain beneath an old rounded beech tree in the garden. A snail slowly, silently, climbs the gnarly truck. Some inner guidance system is leading it to its destination. I feel a strange resonance with that snail. Heart and soul have always done their best to take me where I needed to be. That was once America. Now my inner compass has led me here, to the silence of this place and its resonant invitation to my being. What to do but honour and trust that inner compass to take me home always?

Home is such an evocative word! When I was younger the journey was all about leaving home. In these later years the journey has had more to do with the return. For me, old Scandinavian soul that I am, this has meant a leave-taking of the United States and a returning to Scandinavia.

The road home it seems isn't only travelled once. The journey is an ongoing process. An ongoing spiralling perhaps towards a deepening and opening into ourselves, our gifts and vulnerabilities. This deepening recognition of who we are and what we love seems to involve many a leave-taking, arriving and returning home throughout life. This even if we do not move very far geographically.

Though the influence of place is profound, and though we may be imbued with a sense of belonging in some places that is far greater than in others, ultimately the journey home is always about returning to essence of who we are.

Silent Pulse: A Place Of Resonance

Take yourself to the place
you can hear
the silent pulse of your soul
echo
through the stillness

and pound the drum
of your heart.

Then move on with your life
knowing
you can never live it
quite the way you did before.

Move on
to the rhythm of that pulse
as it reverberates
inside you.

I wrote "Silence" and "Silent Pulse" one directly after the other. They almost feel like one poem. They speak to the importance of finding a place of resonance for heart and soul, where we feel free and invited to listen for and hear something essential about who we are, and how we choose to live our lives.

Longing: A Rendering Of Existence

I drove towards the city
that bright autumnal day
down empty Swedish roads
flanked by granite rock,
pines, a glimpse of sea

I was dreaming of America
once a home to me

a poem came on the radio
it caught me unawares
the words went right in
they spoke of something precious
I had been missing

tears welled and spilled over
as is their wont
when in the presence
of something true about ourselves

eyes blurred and I was forced
to slow down

I had thought the longing was
for that land across the sea
and the life
that I once led there

but then I realised
the yearning was for mirroring
for joining and belonging
with life and with me

I reached my destination
rushed to a café
grabbed a cup of tea
and began to write

how crucial for the heart
to feel
welcome, safe,
reflected and received

a sacred gift
we might offer one another
and ourselves
a listening for the genuine
a recognising and a rendering
of existence
as it is revealed

an inspiration like a poem
on a cold autumn day
in the north

I was in for a surprise, the crisp fall day, I drove into Stockholm, roof down for all the cool of the season. I would like to say with the wind blowing through my hair, that archetypal image, but thanks to an enormous woolly hat, that was not the case. Hurtling down a pale stretch of road a poem came on the radio. It took me by surprise.

Tears did indeed well and spill over. The experience of my heart was reflected in that poem, and my soul felt called to evolve. No wonder once I got to town I had to hare to a café, settle down and write.

Reflecting on that day two things stand out. One, the importance for the heart to feel welcomed, safe, recognised and received. Not just by others but also by ourselves.

The other is perhaps more subtle yet equally important. I could so easily have thought that returning to America, to the place I used to live, would be key for me. Likely not the case. I was no longer really called there, whereas I do now feel called to Sweden. Oh going to the States might have distracted me for a while, but what I really was missing, was in fact right here, in and all around me. Something in me knew, I only needed to remember.

Huddled In The Rain: A Time To Wait

One wet swan
rests between reeds
in the rain
a white orb on grey seas

This is not a time
for sweeping movement
not a time for taking off

This is a time to huddle
head hidden
amidst feathers
aligning intellect with heart
assuaging pain
and incubating promise
a time to be attentive
and to wait

Yesterday's full moon coincided with the storms. Sandy hit the eastern sea board of the United States, whilst here in Sweden wind and rain raged. These are turbulent times, challenging and confronting in many ways.

I think of the swan sheltering between reeds as rain pummels sea and land. I think of her need to lie low, burrowing her head amidst feathers. Perhaps she senses something large is afoot? Something requiring time, and retreat, an allowing of a process to work itself through, for something profound to be reconfigured, before venturing forth yet again?

I saw a satellite image of Sandy in which the configuration of cloud and light at the centre seemed to form a heart, or perhaps even a foetus within a heart-shaped womb, and another in which the central shape seemed to be a yin and yang sign. For all the difficulty and devastation rendered by the storm, some part of me likes to imagine these images as a sort of cosmic message to humanity asking us to evolve and grow in love, open our hearts, rebalance masculine and feminine energies within and around us, and come to live in deeper harmony with existence.

Could It Be The Moon? Called To Evolve

Could it be the Moon
That is causing all this tumult?

Full and overripe
It is churning inner seas
And rendering the world
In sharp relief
Insisting that we see
That we feel
That we acknowledge
Where we are
And what has brought us here.

Could it be the nature of the time?
Threatening, precipitous, demanding,
That will not allow us
To continue as we were?
A time of consequence
And reckoning perhaps?

Could it be that something new
Is emerging?

A time of finding and following
Deep integrity
The essence of who we are
That beckons us to live
In harmony with existence.

Could it be a time
Of relating
With ourselves and one another
The universe and the earth
With a willingness to listen
And respond
To those messages and signs
Our bodies, hearts and souls,
Like this planet
Keep on sending
Begging us to comprehend
What's at stake?

Could it be a time
Of holding faith
With deeper wisdom?

Of honouring earth's call
As we honour our soul's calling
No matter
The requirement to surrender
Who and what and where
We once thought we should be.

Could it be evolution
Is doing something here?
Calling us to waken
To the wisdom of the heart
The knowing of the soul
The insight of the spirit?

To dwell
In examined lives
Rather than in habits?

To give ourselves to love
Rather than to fear?

Are we being asked to choose, now
Between consciousness and calamity?

Meanwhile the moon
Is still pouring light
On the land
Whilst an ocean away
Sandy
The largest tropical storm
Ever recorded above the Atlantic
Batters the eastern seaboard of
The United States.

Wet and wild again today, the weather turbulent like the undercurrent of these times. So much is being questioned and reconfigured! So much we thought we could depend on is no longer to be counted on. What to do but dwell in examined lives, hold faith with deeper wisdom and give ourselves to love?

Fall Reflections: Fragile Beauty

mist rises slowly
sun comes to grace
a distant shore

the green of pines
the yellow of paper birch
revealed

soft reflections
on the surface
of a still
morning sea

oh the wild
fragile beauty of a day

A tender day of feeling fragile…after the storms and all that they involved, comes the vulnerability and a need for stillness. This seems in harmony with the gift of this day. I find a certain comfort in this.

Loss: A Sense Of Sorrow

I look at the apple tree
Its leaves turning
Its once abundant fruit
Mostly plucked or fallen
And feel sad.

How I love that tree.
I have seen it stand stark and naked,
Valiant against a winter's sky.
I have watched it come to blossom
With the spring
Its fruit ripen with the summer
To rosy orbs amidst green leaves
That shone as fall's first golden light
Came to grace them.

Now its aging beauty
With the autumn
Serves to remind me
That many whom I love are aging too.
Fading before my eyes, like the apple tree,
As energy retreats from the outer.

Sometimes to an opening of the heart,
An emotional maturing
A spiritual awakening,

Sometimes to a shrivelling of the soul
Or to a sickness,

Sometimes to an abandonment
Of life itself.

And I cannot shield
Those I love from that journey
Or that loss.

A sense of sorrow befalls me.

What to do
But cherish this moment too?
Know it for what it is
A part of life
Unfolding.

Now as leaves fall from the trees, and the short autumnal days are all but upon us, I feel a sense of loss. Something that befalls all of us at times, whether it be the loss of someone or something dear, the loss of the natural world, or that awful yet sometimes subtle lack of aliveness and joy that comes with a loss of connectedness to our heart and soul.

Yes, there is much to mourn. Yet we may feel afraid of surrendering to our sorrow, of opening the floodgates to torrents of tears, lest we be overwhelmed. It is easy to forget that grieving might be a way to ease the pain and reconnect with heart and soul. Indeed grieving is at times a way to complete things, and we only truly mourn the absence of what we love…

Yes, I want to write about loss. Invite it on to the page. Even in loss there can be beauty. And aging can have its essential wisdom and beauty too. If we are willing and able to stay vital in the sense of staying connected to the heart, the genuine in us, and our spiritual sense.

I have a number of friends well into their seventies and eighties. Some are simply mature. Others have been felled by illness as well, and yet… yet… . Most of them say, unless they are too sick of course, that in many ways these later years are the best of their lives. Here they experience the greatest freedom to be themselves, the greatest freedom from external demand, the greatest sense of attunement with the divine, the greatest insight, and the greatest sense of communion with existence, that sacred joy. I feel to make a wish: may the loss of youth befall us all in this way.

Moon Above A Fir Tree: Beauty In Heartbreak

A fir tree stands sombre and straight
In a silent night.
A full moon comes to hover
just above it,
like a single decoration.

The tree looks so happy,
graced as it now is
by that tender lunar light.
Lit as it now seems
by some secret luminosity
from within.

I can almost hear it singing,
this sweet soft trembling song
whispering right through it.

As the moon slides away
it looks as if the tree is reaching out
begging the moon to stay
or longing just to follow.

Its very essence tilted
by the pull of that still,
reflective face.
Its very being bowed and pining
In a silvery wake.

It appears the tree has been weeping
in the night.

Rainbow-coloured droplets,
like small radiant jewels,
dangle at the end of all its needles.
They shimmer in the early morning glow.

Not a tree of darkness now
But a tree of light.

The dark November days are nearly with us. Energy here in the North is drawing in. Old sorrows and losses are coming up to awareness. In a certain sense you could say this is the season of the broken heart. Or that the ways our hearts are hurting is becoming more clearly revealed.

Trying as this may be, it also has its gifts. Sometimes vulnerability is the thing that lets the soul shine through, leaving us more fragile, yes, but also more luminous somehow and available to life.

The Seal: A Gift Of Communion

I saw the seal today
A dark shadow
Balanced on a rock
Staring right at me

Then the seal slid off the rock
Turned on its side
And raised a flipper
As if to say goodbye
Before diving in
To the deep

I saw the seal today
A radiant being in the water
Waving right at me

A potent reminder
That though we are all
Mysterious and unique
In some essential way
We are connected

And moments
Of communion
Are a gift

I saw the seal today
It seemed a sacred herald
Of the divine

Halloween today. This has long been considered a magical and mystical time. Like all the solar festivals, it is a celebration of the earth's cycle round the sun. We are, now, halfway between autumn equinox and winter solstice. We are, here in the north, about to enter the dark season. As leaves and fruit fall to earth and nature prepares for winter it seems a time to say farewell to all that has passed, that we are ready to surrender.

It is a day, it has been said, when the veil between the spiritual and the mundane may seem particularly thin. It seems of accord with such a day to have seen the seal. To have been graced by its presence and reminded not only of the essential interconnectedness of all things, but also of the need at this time, to wave goodbye to the superficial, and take a dive into the deep.

A Place Of Grace: Falling In Love With The World

A pale sun sifts through the mist
Like candle-light through gauze.
There is a sense of being held
In soft swaddling.

Sea and sky seem as one.
Trees slowly revealed
Display the rosy faces
Of their apples
Amidst yellow fall foliage.

There is a need to be gentle
Go slowly
Stay aligned with the inner
And the simple trust
I will do what I need to
When it needs to be done
Like the beech
Beyond the window
Shedding copper coloured leaves
Because it's time, and they are ready.

I glance out the window and see the soft outline of the apple tree standing in the mist, its apples glowing red against a pearly sky. My heart melts with the simple beauty of this day. I feel brought to my knees. A natural gratitude and reverence for here. May this then be the grace, one of many, of this auspicious time. A falling in love with our world, with the earth, with nature, with ourselves, a falling in love with life. May we know the blessing. May we know ourselves safe and held by nature's gifts, and may we always cherish them.

Winter: Cherishing The Heart

Winter In Andalusia: A Tender Luminescence

Day comes late
Here to the south
And the morning house
Is dark and cold.

Stone walls and marble floors
Hold the chill of night.

Time to light the fire
In the hearth
The candles on the mantle
And settle in
To moments of stillness
Before the dawn.

A soft warmth comes
To grace the heart
A tender luminescence
To touch the being

Both much needed now
After the ferocity
Of a passing yuletide storm.

The holiday season has been intense. Storms have ravaged lands to the north, whilst here in the south the storms have tended to be closer to home. For all the joy of family there have also been challenges on the inner as well as the outer. Something about the intense dark night of an all but moonless winter solstice followed by the birthing of a new moon had me midwifing some crucial aspect of myself and of others as we tended to the child in ourselves and each other. Meanwhile the fire in the hearth kindles the heart and opens me to beauty and to love at a time of all but imperceptible returning light.

Child Within: Essence Of Who We Are

A new kind of peace
Reigns inside me
When I am connected
To my soul child within
To my uniqueness
In harmony with existence
As it unfolds.

When I find myself devoted
To noticing how she feels
Attending to her sorrows
And her joys
Honouring what she loves
As she conveys her wisdom
Through the heart
And through the body
In the present.

A new kind of peace
Reigns inside me
When I am willing to give name
To the pain
Of my wounded child within
The ways she was hurt
And is still hurting.

She needs me to bear witness
And to soothe her
When she gets scared
And reenacts
What she has learned.

Vigilant and dear
She has chosen all along
To do her best to keep me safe.

Yet the hold of the wounded one
Can be too tight
Confining me to a life
Too small
For love and aliveness
To flourish.

A new kind of peace
Reigns inside me
When I am willing to be present
With my inner children
Welcoming and treasuring them both.

And it is to the innocence
Spontaneity and wisdom of my soul child,
I must turn
If I want to be
Connected to the current
And live a life sourced in
The soft grace and joy
The integrity
Of being at one
With her.

I was working with "Child Within" when Agneta Falk sent me a photograph of a painting she had just finished. It was of a child dressed in red, sitting on a step at the entranceway to a large arched grey edifice, looking out over a verdant plentiful land with a river flowing through it.

Looking at Agneta's painting, I found that the barren grey building reminded me of the constructs of the ego. Oh they may have their uses and may help keep us safe, yet being defined by them always comes at a cost.... There can be something cold and lacking in both colour and compassion about them. There is very little joy to be found within their confines.

The child in the picture seems to bring a touch of aliveness to that arid place, as the presence of the inner soul child always will. She is looking out at the beauty and grace of nature and the land.... The child's natural home in the sense of him or her being in harmony with its rhythms and with their own true nature. Indeed the inner soul child is our true nature! Our uniqueness in harmony with and connected to the totality of existence. Child-like but not childish, the inner soul child embodies a certain wisdom and maturity. This is conveyed through feelings, the heart and the body. Connection to my soul child is like a homecoming.

Yes, Agneta your painting touches and stirs me. Could this be the season of the soul child? Is doing the delicate yet crucial work of mending and awakening the heart, that we might feel the presence of the soul child within, the work of this time?

Footprints On The Beach: Interweaving With Life

Waves roll in
and slide up the shore
not quite washing away
the many footprints
left in the sand.

I leave a series of small signs
of my passing,
amidst all the others,

and try for a moment,
such a contrivance!
to fit my footfalls
into those of another
and stumble.

How much grief
we cause
with such distractions!

I return with relief to my natural gait

and glancing behind me
see my tracks,
some deeply etched, some
delicate as the brush of a butterfly wing,
have formed along with the others,
a tapestry of sand.

Waves roll in
and slide up the shore
this time
washing the tapestry away.

How fleeting the chance
to interweave with the world
how precious the possibility.

New Year's Eve, the old year receding, the new one approaching. A chance to ponder what sort of sign of our passing, however fleeting, has been left in our wake? How much have we contrived to walk a path not our own? And what sort of mark, if any, might we make in our lives, and the lives of others, how might we interrelate, this coming year?

What Belongs: Discarding Old Forms

It's that kind of time.
There is a need
For review
For clearing and sorting
A sifting through
Of what encumbers
And of what does not.

What truly belongs
At this stage
Of the journey
And what does not?

What gets to stay poised
On the threshold
Ready for the next step
Of more freely inhabiting
The unfolding mystery
Of our lives?
And what does not?

It's the beginning of the year. Time, tradition has it, of reviewing the old and making resolutions for the new, hence the poem above. What gets to stay poised on the threshold of this New Year, and what does not?

Many are being called to discard old forms that no longer support who they are, on the inner as well as the outer. There is something vulnerable making to this. A phrase I hear over and over these days is "I just don't know".

There is something beautiful and real to this too. Something about being willing to be sensitive to life undefined by old ego ideas but rather surrendered to something more essential, as it unfolds.

When Time Is Ripe: Waiting For Wisdom To Arise

I can't seem to plan much these days.
It's not that sort of time.

Something in me is flummoxed.
I resist making appointments
Unless something deeply
Says yes.

Ambitions and goals are not so alluring.
I am tracking
Something more heartfelt, real, and
Essential to me.

I no longer wish
To be taken
Away from myself
By my strategies.
I want them to support me!

Does this mean I don't fall
Into scheming?
No.
Only that when I make choices
With mind alone,
Or sourced only
In expectations of others,
I become disconsolate.

Better then to delve,
Give space for feeling,
And wait
For wisdom and right action
To arise,

Like some small flower
In spring
Waiting and readying
To blossom, in its own way,
When time is ripe.

I am returned to the North from my sojourn in the South. I am returned to snow and ice and that deep midwinter sense of life, at least on the surface, being on hold.

It was hard to leave Spain. Indeed we did not come back to Sweden, when we had planned. What we had organized did not tally with life as it unfolded in Andalusia. We were quite simply not ready to leave.

How meaningful it can be to stay true to a process rather than attempt to predetermine it. To not be led into a life we do not want by our plans! However, it is not always easy to change them! Not only does most of western culture not work like that, but it can also be quite a process in itself. Old habits of adhering to a schedule (even when the timing is off) may not be easily relinquished! And new agreements with others may need to be made.

Feeling into the rightness of postponing our return was not without issues. However after delving, and waiting for insight to arise, it became clear that postponing our leave-taking, was the most heartfelt thing to do.

Subdued Light: Holding Still

Yet another morning
of no sunshine,
of holding still
and waiting.

These January days
here in the North
are lengthening.
Not so you'd notice.
Such subdued light!

Yet ice skaters scuttle
black clad
on the frozen mottled surface
of the sea,
with its flashes of grey ice here,
and small mounds of old snow there.

The ice makes strange sounds,
half groans, half sighs,
as if not sure it wants
its surface disturbed
by the skaters
who leave it traced through
with little lines.

The earth meanwhile lies nestled
beneath a thin blanket of white
holding still and waiting
for illumination.

A slight headache along with the dark of the day had me wanting to retreat. A friend was to visit. Sensing I needed the day for myself I withdrew from the engagement.

I strongly suspect had I not postponed our meeting, I would not have been in a frame of mind to catch the moment, and this writing would never have come to light.

How often creative process seems to require a withdrawing from the world! How this deep midwinter time seems to invite it, a taking time, like the earth, to rest and regenerate.

Tangling With The Muse: Called By The Creative

When the writing
Is ready
To be poured
Onto the page
And you
Are ready
To receive it
A new poem
Will reveal itself
To you
Replied the Muse
To my worried mind.

I have been tangling with the muse. She has had me for a while now. Not that she always stakes her claim for very long. Sometimes a matter of minutes is all it takes to first form the work on the page.

The wiles of the Muse are not so straightforward though. When she knocks on the door, she will not enter unless duly invited. The call of the muse, the slender threads with which first she tugs on us are not always easy to find or follow, though with time they may become like thick chords, and very compelling.

When these chords come pulling at the heart it is necessary to surrender and go where they wish to take us. For to refuse this allure is costly. The inspiration of the moment may never be found again unless we pay it heed. Just like any lover, the muse once scorned will not so readily return. She must be courted. Her grief at being refused acknowledged. Her welcome must feel secure. However, she does not respond well to the sharing of her gifts on demand. She needs to be ready, and she wants a request that is real.

Clearing a path through which creativity may flow is often needed before settling into the work. This on both the inner and the outer levels of life. This can be a delicious time. Heart and soul know we are getting ready to attend to something they love. The Muse knows space is being made to bid her welcome. A seed of creativity is being held, and ground is being prepared in which to sow it.

How wonderful it is to be taken by creative process! To link heaven and earth through a kind of listening to and receiving of the muse offering her gifts, and bringing them to life. However there is a caution. The process can burn and consume us. When enrapt in its flaming passion, it might cause us to override other needs and feelings that may also be important.

The heart will know what it wants us to do and when, if we will but stop and listen for its subtle messages. It knows when we are ready to receive the Muse and invite her in. Yes tangling with the muse, dancing with her, is a process. As suggested in my poem, inspiration needs to be ready to knock on the door and we need to be ready to receive it.

Holding The Space: Being Attentive To A Process

Some are good at holding the space
At being attentive to a process.

Simply by their presence,
Their listening, receiving and reflecting,
Their ability to accept and wait
For time to be ripe
They are able to create an unseen shelter
In which they and others know themselves
Safe, encouraged, held.

Simply with awareness
They are able to support or partake
In a healing or creative journey
Letting it unfold like a flower
In the sun.

Some are skilled at sheltering themselves
At weaving a container with imperceptible strands
Of consciousness
Inviting insight to arise and feeling to flow.

Holding the space,
Offering a heart-full gracing presence,
A non-doing embrace,
Staying with a process till it's complete,
Is an invisible art
Oft unacknowledged
Yet essential

If we are to cherish life
And encourage love and creativity
To unfold.

There is tremendous beauty in the ability to hold the space and wait for a process to be complete. Yet it is almost an abandoned art. Without the ability to wait nothing would ever have time to grow and come to flower. Life needs the sweet holding of the dark whether it be the dark of the womb, the earth, or the night to mature. It needs time to evolve, so too our hearts and souls. They need the space and time to grow, mend, and become aware, in the context of a simple attentive holding that creates a safe shelter for the process.

One grief of our time is the readiness with which we allow the energetic containers we weave with consciousness, for ourselves or one another, so readily to be shattered. We are a culture of violators and intruders. How fast we are to give ourselves over to too many things, not allowing a process to evolve or come to completion. How little understanding there is of the need for and the grace in holding the space. Yet it is one of the prerequisites not only of a healing or creative process but also of any ongoing intimate relationship. It is a crucial element in the relationship from a parent to a child. And it is a prerequisite of love.

A crucial part of this container making is the willingness to tend and mend the container, with insight and empathy, whenever it has been rent. Yes, this ongoing attentiveness to the energetic space being created, this ongoing mutual response-ability for, and interest in the shared space, is to a large degree what creates a vessel in which the flower of love can blossom.

It might sound a simple practice that of listening, watching carefully, and waiting with awareness for something to be revealed. Yet being attentive to, and current with, a process unfolding, ready to receive or offer the gift of healing, creativity, insight or connection when it comes can be rigorous and demanding. Anyone who has ever held vigil for a loved one will know what I mean. Yet holding the space is at times the greatest gift we can give.

Snow Apples: Welcoming The Heart

red winter apples
gathered on the branch
warming one another
in the snow

their glowing faces
made me think

linger not with those
who do not warm the heart

rather choose to be with ones
offering luminosity
and wanting to surrender
and simply melt

into the sweet sacred sense
of soul
melded with the moment
being offered and received

Yes, linger with those wanting to surrender and simply melt into the sweet sacred sense of soul melded with the moment being offered and received. Linger with those where there is a welcome for the heart.

There is a kind of speaking that can help generate that welcome. This is not a hammering of opinions, judgments or demands designed to keep us from ourselves, one another and deeper knowing, nor is it a litany of the unessential. Rather it is a compassionate naming and a bringing to awareness of what is, without needing to be right.

There is a way of speaking that suggests a willingness to reflect and reveal something genuine, beyond the story of what happened when and to whom. There is a kind of speaking that creates space for silence as well as inspiration.

However when feeling fragile or in the midst of a vulnerable journey on the inner, it may be prudent only to tell someone able to receive you. Otherwise the person's energy or comments may be detrimental to the tender process unfolding within.

There is a kind of listening, a compassionate non-doing witnessing and presence, a willingness to receive and let things be, that invites a co-creative deepening in to the moment and imbues it with connectedness and meaning.

There is a way of being in conversation that invites insight, and yes, even love, to arise. Love flows when we feel safe to connect and be real. It falters when we feel attacked, diagnosed, judged, threatened or unsafe. It can take so very little for the heart to shrivel or shut down in self-defence and for soul – who we essentially are – to cringe.

Yes, I want, when I can, to be with ones wanting to invite a little warmth into the room and partake of something fundamental. I want, when I can, to make a welcome for the heart, and offer it a chance to glow.

Two Deer: Tender Relating

It has snowed again overnight.
Several inches deep,
it lies mounded over fence posts,
balanced precariously
on thin branches of trees,
and continues to fall silently
through the still air.

We must go for a walk.
My beloved and I.
The path is beckoning.

We plan to walk up the hill first,
have it behind us,
but coming to the hill we see
a clutch of neighbours chatting.
Preferring stillness on this day,
the simple union of two hearts
open and vulnerable
beating with love,
we turn to the left instead.

In a moment, two delicate deer
prance lightly through veils of snow,
across the road before us.

Young, unsteady on their legs,
shy and elusive, like soul seems to be,
they turn to face us, eyes alert,
ready for flight in an instant.

We stand communing
for a fragment of time.
It seems they have a message.

Be gentle with yourselves
tender and forgiving.

An undefended heart is a fragile thing.

With its presence you'll be blessed
with warmth and grace and love.
But it will retreat in a moment
if you do not tend it well,
and the magic
will be lost.

Yes be sensitive to yourselves
and one another
and we will come…in the quiet
when defences are all down
and you feel safe
to dance a simple dance,
of freedom, grace and love.

Deeply moved we wander on
through untracked snow.

How susceptible the unshielded heart!

How finely tuned and receptive
love's gift calls us to be,

How tenderly
we are invited to relate.

In a world that often considers it cool to be tough, I want to make a plea for the opposite. I want to bring awareness to the gift of tender relating – sharing and connecting with the heart felt, without the need to attack or be defensive. I want to honour the gift in being safe to be open, vulnerable and real, available for a rich experience of daily life – able to be moved by the sight of two deer crossing the road. I want to honour the gift in being available for and vulnerable to love. Love flows when we feel safe and attracted to connect. It falters when we don't.

Cupid's Arrow – A Poem Of Love

I want to write about love, that tender elation,
Fruit of being with the beloved…

I want to say that being with the loved one is a
    journey,
Is a present, quite unlike any other. It will ask
that you discard everything that isn't really you.
That isn't truly of your heart.
That doesn't genuinely convey
Who you are.

In return it will offer everything. A vital and attractive
    sense
Of safety and communion in which the soul is free
To discover, come forward, and be.

To maintain this silken effervescence, this gentle joy,
Empathy and kindness towards oneself will be needed,
Empathy and kindness towards the other too.

There is a need to tend the union with oneself.
There is a need to tend the union with the other.
There is a need to tend the union with the creative.
There is a need to be free to tend all three.
Love only flows when we feel free.

Yes the gift of love is precious. A sanctuary
In which the heart is invited to be real.
This is a place to be cherished.
Loves moment can so easily be lost
If we do not tend it well.

Any rough word, criticism, or command
Will likely close the heart.
Connection cannot happen when a heart is fortified.
And love cannot flow without connection.

Love's warmth washes through the body,
Through the psyche, sometimes flushing
All the hidden places of agony, anger, grief,
To the surface, to be given over
To the light of recognition.

This can be a painful process
Challenging at times
Yet it is also what can help
Love to flow.

It's not for nothing Cupid's arrow is said to pierce the heart.
It is perhaps this very penetration that can shatter the defences,
And open us to feeling and communion?

Yes, I want to write about love.
The sacred gift of being with the beloved…
A natural blessing bestowed on lovers by existence.

Valentine's Day yesterday. Seemed a good day to write about love.... Love between people of course, but for me love can also be about love of nature, the planet, the divine, communion with existence, one's work, a particular place...anything that is a heart-full calling and a true path.

Any kind of genuine love will likely awaken similar processes. We may feel graced by inspiration, insight, gratitude, growth and joy. We may also be touched by pain and challenge. We may come face to face with the places our heart has been closed to ourselves, to the beloved, or to existence. For this is part of love's gift: revealing and supporting the soul's purpose and what it loves, as well as healing that which impedes love's true expression.

An Umbrella Of Compassion: Cherishing The Heart

A slow Saturday afternoon.
Rain. Damp wood on the fire.
Snow and ice melting.

Long lines of droplets
On twiglets on trees
And me marching along
Wondering how best to treasure
What is precious deep inside?
How best to stay connected
To the current?

Surely not by becoming like a fortress,
Or by shutting down?
Surely not by building up
A mental armoury
Or by assuming battle garb?

NO!!! Even though I still may don them,
I don't want to become good at bearing suits of mail.

Not after all these years of longing – of working –
For those old suits to soften,
For my battle dress to crack or melt,
That love might shine right through.

For love
Surely is the best defence.
Casting fields of love
Round all that is hurting,
All I care for and more…

Rain bounces off the rim of my hat
Sprinkling my cheeks.
I wipe the cold little droplets away.

Yes. Surely being loving
Kindly towards myself and others
Holds a key?

Being patient and forgiving.
Alert to my process.
Trusting the wisdom
Of the heart.

I imagine myself dancing
Beneath an umbrella of heart-fullness
Kindness and compassion
And soon find myself back home.

With the curtains drawn
And fire rekindled,
I start to think
About following my heart
And inhabiting my life.

It seems to require such fortitude and faith.
In a world that always is so greedy
For something more, or else.
It seems to require
That I remember my umbrella…

I have found remembering that heart-full umbrella of compassion helps bring me ease when feeling anxious or upset. Small kindly conversations – even imaginary ones – with myself or others, help soothe body and soul and help me proceed about my way more wisely. They encourage me to drop out of an agitated mind and come into the heart. Particularly when I imagine sending love to difficult situations. A smile comes to my face as I write this, indicating my heart is happy and agrees. It likes it when I include it and remember, when needed, to hoist my umbrella.

The Heart Awakens: Being Response-Able

The heart awakens
Its responsiveness exquisite.
It closes in a moment
When not welcomed,
recognised and safe.

It closes to that not in accordance
With what the deeper part of us
Knows, longs for, needs, and loves.

It closes when we don't
Hold ourselves with compassion.

The heart numbs
Its responsiveness defiled or curtailed

By violation or old wound.

The heart awakens
Its responsiveness exquisite
It opens in a moment
When welcomed, recognised, and safe.

When we hold ourselves
With compassion.

It opens to that which resonates
With what the deeper part of us
Knows, longs for, needs and loves,

That which makes us glad to be alive.

The heart awakens
Its responsiveness exquisite.

This poem says something about how it feels to be connected to the heart. It says something about the delicious wisdom and spontaneity of its flow. It knows when it is safe to show its face, and when it is not. A messenger of the soul it is a wonderful companion and guide if we choose to welcome its presence and honor what it knows. There is an immediacy to its wisdom: its feelings of pain as well as joy, hard if not impossible to experience with the mind alone.

In difficult times the heart is one of the best guides and supports we can find, particularly when we are willing and able to receive and interpret its responses accurately.

The Heart Opens: The Gift Of Vulnerability

The heart opens
Vulnerability enters
Like an arrow
Unspeakable joy
Irrepressible pain

The heart bruised
Yet beating

I make my confession
This transgression or that
This agony or that

The solace of recognition
Of grief given its rightful name
The unbearable made bearable
Again

The heart opens
Vulnerability enters
Like an arrow
Irrepressible pain
Incredible insight
Unspeakable joy

The "Heart Opens" came the other day. It speaks about the beauty and the sorrow inherent in an opening of the heart…in an opening to feeling.

The heart opens and is smote by the sight of a small dog, in a cage at the airport, going round and round on a baggage carousel, and no one comes to claim him. The heart opens and softens at the sight of a loved one, walking slowly across the sparking snow-covered lawn, in the early morning light. Tears well at the extraordinary beauty, strength, generosity, and fragility of life…and with grief when this sacred gift is defiled.

The heart opens vulnerability, that silent strength enters as a softening, exposing us to sorrow, inner wisdom, and to joy.

Tears Come Easily: Susceptible To Life

Tears come easily
These days.

A beloved pine
Being felled
To make way for a road,
A picture of a place
I used to live,
Or of someone I loved
No longer here,
The sight of my honey
After even the briefest
Of sojourns,
An act of kindness
One person to another,

The natural beauty
Of something true and en-souled,
Brings tears.

Grief and relief intermingled
The sorrow of loss
The joy of reunion.

Someone once said,
"You can tell when a person
Is in the presence of themselves,
Because they cry."

Yes, tears come easily
These days.
Sign
Of an increasing
Susceptibility, to life.

A gentle day today of snow falling softly beyond the window. A day to curl up by the fire, read a novel and write. It seems a day to welcome the vulnerable, the receptive, the susceptible. A day to connect with old sorrows and, with an accurate naming, soften around them and let the tears flow. It is a day of simple pleasures too.

Yes, I feel to welcome the gift of the tears when they come, sometimes with a look of sorrow and sometimes with a smile. They are an expression of an opening in to myself, to connectedness and love.

I am grateful for this increasing sensitivity that is perhaps a hallmark of aging. It can take a deal of inner strength as well as a sense of safety to connect with the heart, feel, be vulnerable and real, and let the tears fall when they will.

Listen: When Everything Feels Too Much

When worries come to plague you in the night
Listen to your deeper knowing

When you want to tear your hair out
In despair
Not knowing what to do
Listen to the voice of the one
In you who knows
It is not all your fault
And not yours alone to solve this

When the burdens feel too big for you to bear
Feel the fear, feel the grief, and surrender
To the place in you that resonates
With the silent pulse
Of your soul

Yes
When everything feels too much
Listen to the wisdom of your heart

I wrote LISTEN after one of those nights of waking with the worries at four AM.... Wanting, and needing to soothe myself, I placed my hand on my heart, and taking several deep breaths asked for its wisdom to be revealed.

I found this deeply consoling. It helped me return to a deeper truth underlying my anxiety. It reminded me rather than trying to control everything to feel safe, to remember my umbrella of compassion and imagine it protecting me. To have faith in the process, and surrender to heartfullness.

How To Be Gentle: The Soft Voice Of The Soul

she asked me
how to be gentle with herself
how to listen for
the voice of the soul
this was my reply

stay with your energy and your flow
let yourself go slow

promise you will cherish
your wise and tender heart
affirming what it feels

say something soothing to yourself
say "I understand…"
say "you have been forgiven"
say "I love you…"

do not be afraid
of entering the silence
though sometimes this is where
your pain will be revealed
it is also where your wisdom oft resides…

this is where the soft voice of your soul
may be heard

so stay with your energy and your flow
and let yourself go slow.

Snow is falling beyond the window. A brief flurry perhaps before spring finally takes hold? Its Easter vacation in Sweden and the world fittingly is still. Seems a good moment to remember to be gentle. To surrender to the silence, letting the quiet joy in doing nothing enfold me, and grace me with the simple gift of allowing my being to flower, like the daffodil standing on the sill.

Midwinter Still: Pregnant With Possibility

A strong wind
In from the south
Brings sullen skies,
Rain, and melting snow.

It soughs through trees.
Their keening echoes
Round the old granite rocks
Whose faces, wet with weeping,
Are revealed too soon
Now they have lost
Their white winter mantles.

Even the sea looks surly.
Great grey puddles
Depress its frozen form.

No one ice-skates today.
And the lanes
Awash with slush on ice
Are treacherous to walk.

Nothing to do but stay in and wait.
Nothing I want to do
Even in retreat.

The mind is quick to judge.
"What is wrong with you?"

The reply is obvious:
"Nothing."

For all the thaw this is not
The burgeoning uprush of spring.
This is the pregnant waiting time

Of deep midwinter still.

It is deep midwinter still. Yes, this is the nature of the time. Down in the earth little seeds may be stirring yet, here in the north, they are far from ready to reveal their faces.

This is a time pregnant with possibility not yet ready to be revealed. The nothingness of this time is not devoid of life. In a certain sense it holds, and nourishes the very essence of it. It is a time of waiting. Of allowing soul, or a healing and creative process, to unfold.

Many a time I have found that if I refuse to enter the nothingness, I do not receive its gift. Indeed this is often the hardest part of any creative journey, the carving out of the space for nothing. Allowing it, surrendering to it.

The old habits of filling the space, even when home alone can be easy to slip into. Not everyone understands when I say, "I am very busy doing nothing. Please do not disturb." As a culture we may not be willing to offer or take this kind of time, nor is it always comfortable, but certainly it is rewarding, necessary and real.

Even when out and about I find it important to stay cherishing of the process that is unfolding in the deep. Cherishing of my nothingness. This includes staying alert to the vagrancies of the mind. How quick its acculturated voice can be to condemn. Though a useful aspect of ourselves particularly when operating in service of soul, it is usually better not to let our thoughts alone define who we are, but rather listen to and honour what our deeper heartfelt wisdom already knows.

Mending Nets: Receiving Deeper Wisdom

Two old ice-fishermen trudge frozen seas
Making their way home
In the rain.

Two small sleds filled with tackle
Trail behind them
On wet and puddled ice.

It's been said when the weather
Is too wild for fishermen
To go to sea
They mend nets.

This is just such a time.
Conditions are inclement.
There is a need to be home
And mend
The fabric of the heart
Where it's been rent.

Snagged yet again
By some old fear or form
Some outcrop of the past
Some quaking of the present
Some worry of the future.

There is a need to repair
To reweave the inner
With awareness and with love.

Make it delicate, flexible, strong,
Ready to receive the catch
When it comes

Of realization, wisdom, creativity and love,
Receive the silent pulse of the soul,

These offerings from existence
To a heart
Ready now and waiting

Like those fishermen
To return to the sea.

Rain has turned to snow beyond the window. White-out conditions prevail. The far shore, invisible now, seems a metaphor for these times. This is not exactly a visionary moment. It's more a time for tending the being. For all the returning light, and the first stirrings of new creative energy, it is winter still.

There can be a need to go slowly and mend the heart where it's been rent that we might deepen into the moment, connect with the current and give life to that which wants to emerge with the spring.

Thinking Of Snowdrops: Dropping Ambition

An small breeze blows across the surface
of a still frozen sea.
It cajoles sullen mounds of snow
into melting
and dances round
the first snowdrops of the year.

Those small hardy souls taken by a dream
have been on a journey
through rough and freezing ground,
and now they are here.
Leaves and stalks protected
by a remnant of old snow,
their closed waxen heads
tossing with the wind.

Nothing now for them to do
but wait
trusting earth and snow to hold them,
and sun and rain to grace them.

Nothing to do but let go
of the ambition
to get ahead
and make it to the surface.

Nothing to do
but soften and allow themselves
to be with the moment
and open when they will.

I think of the first small snowdrops of the year and their journey just to get here. I think of their drive to plough through rough earth and show their faces to the sun. I notice there is a need for them to surrender that old thrust, once bathing in the light, and simply let their beauty blossom.

Their surrender into being seems a matter of both illumination, readiness and maturity. And I wonder if we, personally and collectively, are standing on the threshold of illumination, readiness and maturity? Are we like those snowdrops rooted in the deep, being called to honour the season and let ourselves be in harmony with existence as it unfolds?

A Small Swan Tear: Grief And Relief

Now after the night frost
The morning land looks cold
And ice still covers
The surface of the sea.

And yet, birds are singing brightly
Heralding the spring
And twigs are all asparkle
With drops of melting frost
And the swans...Swans!
First sighting this year
Flying low and honking
Over the water's frozen form,
Searching for, and not finding,
Open water on which to land.

And I wonder if the ice on the trees
Turning to water
Has a moment of mourning the loss
Of its crystalline form
As it celebrates the softening
Into liquid?

I wonder if the swans
Mourn the loss of open ocean
And worry that the sea, here
Is not yet ready to receive them
Leaving them hovering
In that awkward place between worlds
Where the old has been left,
And it still is not clear

Whether the new
Will welcome them?

And I wonder if small swan tears fall
As they fly and instinctively turn,
Not back whence they came, but to the left,
Round yonder island
To where, yes, open water now flows…

I wonder if landing there,
Another tear falls
Of love, longing, loss, intermingled,

A tear of grief and of relief

In recognition of

The real.

I want to write about grief. Who wants to read about that? We have become feeling phobic as a culture. We don't want to know our true responses. Don't want to know our true pain or our true joy. We prefer the high, the numb, the pretended. We want to pretend that happy or unperturbed is how we are. That unlike the moon we are full on all the time when in reality, like the moon, we have cycles and seasons, a need for dark and retreat as well as a need to shine. We pretend that we, existing in worlds that do not encourage or sustain us, really are OK.

There have always been those in positions of authority, who are skilled at ways of shaming and manipulating what we feel. Always been those who are served by disallowing feeling that we might meet their needs and demands. This whether they be in churches, in governments, in corporations, in schools, or in families. And we have become good at internalizing and repeating their voices peppering our conversations and inner dialogues with words of attack, criticism, shame, demand, and blame.

Oh yes we have become good as a culture at creating shame in association with who we are and what we feel, and guilt in association with what we do. We seem to ignore, not to value or encourage the innate ethical sense of what is fair, decent and true. We look to replacing a sense of integrity, justice, beauty, empathy, generosity, and curiosity, along with a desire to contribute to the whole and make it better, in each our unique way, with a set of rules, oughts, shoulds and untrue dictums. Yet this innate ethical sense is a crucial inner compass and guide. An inner compass so often left lost and buried beneath the norms, demands, expectations and emotional wounds, that caused us to discard it in the first place.

There is, perhaps no greater grief than the willful overriding of this inner wise place inside and the willful suppression of our feelings. You can see that lack of aliveness, and responsiveness to life, in too many faces. You can see the frozen condemnation, the embedded hatred, anger, resentment, or sorrow at the loss of something essential. You can see it in the manic high, the fake smile, the forced enthusiasm and joy. You can feel it in the atmosphere around certain people. Hear it in their judgmental unkindly, and yes at times frankly toxic, behaviours and words.

Yes. Time to start the work of reclaiming our inner compass! It's time for an awakening of the heart. With this awakening comes not only joy but also pain. It is as if all the places we have been ripped from the essence of ourselves are crying out to be mended, and this can be painful. It's no wonder we refuse it. Stop ourselves from feeling by keeping busy, or by using mood-altering substances or pills. There is so much to grieve, so much to let go of or change, personally and collectively, particularly now when the world seems wrought through both with peril and with promise.

Of course we are afraid of opening the floodgates to torrents of tears. No one told us this is a natural part of the healing journey. There is nothing wrong in feeling sorrow. Indeed at times it is both healthy and wise! So of course at times we want to weep. Why wouldn't we? Indeed not to may only be a way of perpetuating numbness, the madness, and the pain. May only be a way of not realizing what we love, and may only be a way of negating our true joy. Yes joy.

For underneath sorrow there is profound joy in existence, in living, in being alive. Do we really want to refuse this too?

To be alive is to constantly change and evolve, or not.

Each moment is new. There is a constant surrender of what was, a constant opening to what is a constant unfolding of what will be... a constant chance, to open to our feelings recognize and allow their wisdom to unfold.

Yes, I have wanted to write about grief, to invite it onto the page and invite the heart to open, not only to sorrow but also to relief, and to joy just as I liked to imagine was the case for those swans in my poem.

Spring: Sourced In Inner Wisdom

Betwixt And Between: Waiting For Hidden Life To Take Form

Dank and drear today
A low mist hovers
Over a grey
And sullen sea.

A patchy dusting of snow
Vies for position
On the lawn.

Meanwhile the trees
Stand laden with the damp.
Small droplets hang on twigs,
Unsure whether to hold on or let go.

Uncertain of their fate if they surrender
And let themselves fall
To the wet and muddy earth below
Rife with flecks of snow
And last season's rotting leaves
Yet dotted with small green shoots of spring.

Which season is this?
I want to hibernate again.
Hold the covers close
Cocooned from winter's undertow
And let hidden life take form
As I wait

For the emergent star
To rise across the heavens
And melt the outmoded
So I may surrender
Yet again
To love's warming light.

Let go, like those droplets might
And merge with budding life unfolding.

It's that kind of time, betwixt and between the seasons. It is a time of waiting. The old not ready to let go, the new not yet fully formed. There can be a sense of impatience. Enough already! However the waiting time is sacred too. It is pregnant with possibility. If we don't allow the waiting what is unfolding will be born premature and we will suffer the grief of loss and unfullfillment as something emerges before it is ready to be lived. Better then to be like the daffodils, sheathed in green in their pot on the step, waiting as yet to show their yellow faces to the sun.

Not As It Seems: A Deeper Truth

Small frozen ripples
On the surface
Of the sea

Motion solidified

How beguiling they are
At first glance
The water seemed
Ice free

I am reminded
Not to be
So quick to judge

A deeper truth
Often underlies
A first perception
Of reality

The ice covering the surface of the sea has gone now. Indeed this morning looking out I expected to see open water. However…not the case. A heavy frost in the night caught the water unawares, freezing little wavelets in place. Days now may be longer than the nights. However, here at 60 degrees North, winter has not yet entirely relinquished its hold.

Meanwhile another reflection engages me: that of not being so quick to judge. Not least people. Mostly when someone seems angry, or unpleasant, or I feel annoyed, some sort of unhappy back story is taking place. Some sort of worry or trouble, or pain is besetting them, or me! I am reminded again to leave my umbrella of compassion open and not be quite so quick to judge the other or myself. Things are not always the way that they seem to be at first glance. A deeper truth does indeed often underlie reality.

Screens Of Smoke: The Mind Starts

The mind starts
Its endless ranting.

It's easy to get hooked
By its demands, judgments,
Fears and decrees,
Smokescreens devised
To keep me from myself.

Screenes of smoke
Mostly bequeathed me by others
With notions of what I should do
And how I should be
Swirl
Through my head.

Words bequeathed me by a friend
Swirl
Round my heart:

"Pushing people beyond their authenticity
Damages them."
I am vulnerable today.
Better not to push myself
Beyond it.

Better to acknowledge
The feeling,
Than defend against it
With notions not attuned
To a deeper part
Of me.

Better to soothe the soul
With deeper wisdom.
A remembering of all
I am so grateful
For.

The mind starts
Its endless twirling.

Better to be still
Hold myself
With compassion
And tend the messages
My heart wishes to convey
And receive.

I wrote the poem above when I was beset by the mind running round and scaring me with its need to judge, dominate, take control, fix me, and lead me to a life I did not want, with little or no regard for the heart, for deeper wisdom, presence and what actually wanted to unfold.

Time to take a breath and remember what I love about my life, and in the gratitude of that remembering be returned to my heart and to feeling. Time to take a breath and remember words once proffered me by Jeanne Mayell: "Pushing people beyond their authenticity damages them." How true and perhaps one of the great emotional wounds so many of us bear at this time.

You Can't Get There From Here: A Matter Of Surrender

You can't get there from here.
You can't get to a sense
Of aliveness and connection,
Those simple joys,
By being invulnerable.
Or from striving to be
Who or what you think
You should.

You can't get there
From the place in your heart
Once ravaged, that you closed
To any comprehension
Or awareness of how you really feel.
The place that keeps your essence obscured
Even from you.
You can't get there
Whilst hostage to an emotional wound
Or from being at war.

Empathy is needed for that.

No, you can't get
To the soft luminosity of life
That breaks your heart
And opens you to love
By being obedient
Or by acting out.
This light lives beyond
All that.

You can however get there
From bringing a glow
Of awareness and compassion to your pain
From grieving what you lost
From being vulnerable.

You can get there
From the simple act of surrender
To what you deeply sense
To what you deeply love.

You can't get there from the mind alone
But you can
From the unveiling of the heart.

As soon as I saw the painting *You Can't Get There From Here* by Debora House, I knew that there was a poem in there somewhere. Putting pen to paper I began to write and the poem above emerged.

There is a tendency to think that if we do more, or try harder, we will be able to experience that subtle sense of joy at the core of our being that underlies everything. There can be a hope that if we are good enough or rebel enough or are precocious or assertive enough, or successful enough something wonderful will happen.

No, not in terms of this softening into ourselves and existence. That sweet communion is more a matter of surrender into the moment, into what we really love, and what truly brings us joy, than it is the result of a battle with ourselves to be what we are not. In a world that often seems so focused on our proving ourselves at any cost, we may do well to remember that an opening of the heart, rather than an attempt to inform it of how it ought to feel or be, may well have the more profound effect.

A Butterfly Waits: Trusting The Process

A caterpillar crawls along a leaf
Gorging on the greenery
Sated, the larva cocoons itself on a twig.
The cocoon hardens into a chrysalis
Where new cells, called imaginal disks,
Begin to form.

The larva sensing a threat, to its survival
Attacks and consumes them.
Undaunted, the imaginal disks
Keep on coming.

As the caterpillar dissolves into a soup,
The imaginal disks link together
Co-creating the emergent,
Evolving into a butterfly.

This may be such a time.
Personally and collectively
We may be in the soup
Of transition!
The old may be in question.
The new neither formed nor in place.

No good trying to stay a caterpillar
When a butterfly is waiting to be born!
No good clinging to old forms
Or attacking them.
If you join them,
They are likely to consume you.

No good attacking the emergent
Or, with caterpillar consciousness,
Pretending to be a butterfly.

Better to let awareness and love
Melt the outmoded
And accept the dissolution
When it comes.

Feel the pain, allow the grief,
Find and follow the imaginal,
However vulnerable and small
The first essential movement,
And become a beacon
In dark times.

This is a healing journey
An evolution of consciousness
An inhabiting of integrity
And compassion.

Better then to trust the process
Than resist it!
Cocoon ourselves when needed
In harmony with existence
And wait
For wisdom to be revealed.

Better then to live what we love
And join with others
Consciously engaged
In cherishing the inner butterfly
And awakening
The heart of the world.

I was inspired to write "A Butterfly Waits" when my husband asked me how I was feeling. I heard myself reply, "Well I am 'in the soup.' Like a caterpillar in a cocoon. I don't yet know what this transition will bring. I am in the mystery."

We then fell into talking about how this may not just be a personal process, but a collective one as well. Many of us sense the unsustainability of our current ways of life. We know, or sense, that what we have been doing to ourselves, one another and the planet, is sourced in habitual patterns of survival.

We may intuit that these patterns have created a false sense of self, symbolized by the caterpillar, and built by ourselves and others to survive in a culture founded on fear, scarcity, disconnectedness, narrow-mindedness, dominance, submission, control, and power over, rather than on love, sufficiency, connectedness, integrity, mutuality, freedom, self-organization, and an innate ethical sense.

We may feel, the essential mystery of the butterfly, symbol of an authentic self, in and around us, is beginning to unfold and is wanting to co-create a culture sourced in love. We may not know exactly what this evolutionary process will look like. Indeed to seek to define it too soon is a ravage, as we are likely to define ourselves, with the consciousness of the caterpillar rather than with the vision and awareness of the butterfly.

Yet we may feel the call in our hearts just the same. We may feel the call of the imaginal to awaken and connect with the imaginal in others, however hard the journey. We may feel the call to co-create and transition, with acknowledgement to the caterpillar for its contribution, into the beautiful, unique, sensitive yet resilient, butterflies we may be becoming...

Poem first published in the Swedish magazine *Om Omstallning* (About Transition)

Mouse Ears: Listening For Inspiration

Tiny birch leaves – mouse ears – cling
To the tree's trailing branches
Forming a wafting curtain
Around the resting deer

Sheltering it
From the intensities of the world
And warning it
Should danger come too close

I find at times I want
A mouse ear curtain like that
To protect
The vulnerable in me
From overstimulation and demand

Life simplified
That I may listen for and hear
Small insightful messages
In the shelter

Of those wafting branches
With their little mouse ear leaves…

May 1st, today, half way between spring equinox and summer solstice. A day tradition has it in the north of celebrating spring. As if in affirmation of this a Swedish friend, Agneta Falk, sent me a photo of Ohm Mountain partially hidden behind what she described as a drape of tiny birch leaves, known as mouse-ears.

As soon as I received it I knew there was a poem in there somewhere. Combining her image with memories of the garden where I live, I found myself writing the poem above and would like to share it here with you.

Beckoned By The Moon: Called By The Feminine

a full moon hangs
close to the horizon
in a blue predawn sky

it casts
a luminous path
across the surface
of the sea

and beckons to the heart
like a poultice
on a wound
to release its pain

and surrender
to the presence

of that soft lunar light
as it conjures, soothes and delights
yet again

There are those, and I am one of them, who like to think of the moon as a symbol of a sound inner feminine. A symbol of the receptive, the reflective, the listening, the sensing, as well as the intuitive aspect of ourselves. The relational if you will. The part of us able to hold and receive the feelings and knowing of the inner child as well as a more transpersonal awareness referring to people, places, situations or insights beyond the immediacy of the child.

The inner feminine connects and soothes as she, like the moon, adheres to her path. Journeying with the mysteries of life as they unfold, she bathes them in a tender light, a light of wisdom, of insight and of love. Though should a situation require it, her light can be both steadfast and strong.

Like the moon escorted by the stars, the inner feminine escorted by the masculine – the part of us that expresses, analyses, strategises, constructs and takes action, stays true to her rhythms and her seasons. No wound, nor grace, does she counter with her forgiving light.

Hearts soften in her silvery glow. Minds cease their endless chattering. Relieved spirit dances when she pours compassion onto persons parched and thirsting for her luminosity.

The gift of her presence can be like a poultice on a wound, drawing out pain, and offering comfort. Without her we would never know who we are, or what we love. Without her, essence would not be received or revealed, and we would never know the present that would quench our deepest thirst.

The feminine holds a secret source within. Part in shadow like the moon, she weaves mysteries no one sees. Her deepest communion is often when she is dark: when she has turned away to retreat, and to retrieve the magic of her soul or make ready to respond, when the calling comes, to receive, intuit, distill, muse, mirror, enlighten and unfold the essential in herself, in others or in existence, before moving on.

Yes, I like to think of the moon as a symbol of the inner feminine…I am grateful to have seen that round lunar face, in a blue predawn sky. It called me to remember the grace of the feminine and her sacred gifts.

Like A Peony: Remembering The Grace Of The Feminine

how wonderful to feel
the warmth of sun
shining on my back

to saunter
rather than power-walk
with Nordic poles
along the lanes

to breathe in
the fragrance of blossoms
on fruit trees
of lilacs their fonds hanging over
someone's fence
showering me with petals
as I pass beneath

how wonderful to hear the nightingale sing
in the thicket
the cuckoo cuckoo
in the forest
and see
the pheasant stand stately and proud
by the hedgerow
whilst two white butterflies
dance
right above him

how wonderful to sashay
like some middle-eastern dancer
hips swaying, hands lifting
with life's invisible lilt
and this oh
so subtle sense
of earth energy rising

opening me to life
like the many petalled peony
blossoming in the garden

how wonderful
after so many months
of feeling driven
to surrender yet again
to the grace of the feminine
and the gifts of mother earth

This poem seems to reflect the energy of the moment, at least for me. Yes, I am sensing the shift, a surrender into the grace of the feminine and a more receptive approach. This feels quite frankly not only wonderful, and like a sweet relief, but also as though it may be crucial. Perhaps this really is a time in which we are called personally and collectively to find ways of living on this planet that cherish, rather than exploit, the earth's sacred gifts, as well as our own, including the gifts of the feminine?

Do Not Forget: Tend Yourself, Tend The Earth

Do not forget
That as you tend yourself
You tend the Earth

She celebrates every moment
Of your joy
And suffers every moment
Of your pain

She is your perfect mirror
Just as you are hers.

She shows you
Where your heart
Has become distorted

And you no longer know
What you really want
Or are able to appreciate
What really matters.

She shows you
Where your heart
Has opened to love

And reflects your ability
To cherish
The sacred challenge and the gift

Of life
On planet Earth.

The poem above came in meditation. It came with the insight that truly tending myself is a way of tending life on earth, and so perhaps also the very Earth itself? This is indeed a time of challenge for the planet and for humanity. Will we come to cherish the gift of life on earth in time?

Tangles Of Wild Flowers: Energy Is A Form Of Intelligence

today little energy
for ironing
paying bills, doing taxes
or running errands
little energy
for emails, writing
speaking with friends
little energy for work

then I realized
I had energy aplenty
for walking tree-lined lanes
edged with tangles of wildflowers

I had energy aplenty
to amble
through dappled sunlight
the air soft and warm
on bare arms and legs
as I realised

vitality is
moment to moment
a precise guidance system

aliveness is found
sometimes
in a simple act
of walking or resting
sometimes it's engendered by necessity

sometimes it is found
in an act of creation
and sometimes…

energy is
a form of intelligence

it was not that I'd had little
more
I'd simply not understood
where my energy
wished
to take me

A mix of sun and rain beyond the window. First one and then the other, back and forth. The weather, like me, unable to decide. For the weather, rain or sun? For me a trip to the city this afternoon to meet a friend, or not? This may seem a small decision. Indeed it is. Yet I need to let her know if I am to cancel, and the process of making this choice harkens to other larger ones.

Sitting by the phone about to call her I feel unsettled. What shall I say? Wise words once spoken by my American friend Lily come to mind. "I have found," she said, "that desire to do something is no longer enough for me to choose to do it. I also need to check if I have I the energy, and whether or not it is a priority."

Desire, energy, and priority." Lily's words echo in my head. "Desire, energy, and priority." Helpful to investigate when needing to make a choice.

On this day that investigation revealed I just did not have enough energy for a trip to the city. A smile came to my face. I felt a sense of relief. Often signs that I am on the right track. So I called my friend. In that wonderful way that often happens when staying true to energy and flow, it turned out she would also rather not meet today. We decide to honour and husband our energy and agree to speak on the phone instead.

Cows: Freedom, Spontaneity And Delight

Cows frolic in a field
After long winter months
Confined to their stalls.

Prancing and jumping
They enthuse about life
With such sweet abandon

Tears well as I watch them
And I wonder:

What
Keeps us confined
To a life too small
For aliveness and joy?

And what
Might we need,
Like those cows
To regain a sense
Of freedom, spontaneity and delight?

Tradition has it here in the North of celebrating the day when finally it is warm enough for the cows to be released into fields of green from their winter captivity in the barns. Their wonderful spontaneous delight is something to behold. If you have never witnessed it, I highly recommend it.

There is something about spontaneity, isn't there? It speaks to me of a connectedness not only to the instinctual but also to the heart. I notice how spontaneously tears might arise, how immediate can be the smile or the frown, how empathetic the heart can be in any given situation? The heart knows. All I have to do is recognize its wisdom.

Indeed I have come to trust those spontaneous tears, smiles and frowns in response to situations or ideas. I find them a useful guide. There is however an important point to be made here. The natural spontaneity of the heart in which the immediacy of its wisdom is expressed may sometimes be confused with the reactivity of a wounded heart.

Though they may appear similar there is in fact a huge difference between them. The responsiveness of a wise heart is pure spontaneity and an expression of our aliveness. It has not been debauched or deadened by emotional wounds and does not distort its responses, or spew unconstrained toxicity. Unlike the wounded heart, a heart that is wise reveals where the source of our freedom, spontaneity and delight truly lies, and encourages us to bring them to life.

School Children: Waiting To Blossom

School children wait
In shelter after shelter
For the bus

They look uniform and bleak

I hope they won't be shuttled
To a school of a kind
That is a holding pen
For fledglings

Where they will be managed and prepared
However subtly or overtly
To enter a daily grind

A place where creativity
Aliveness, vision and diversity
Often is consumed

And unique minds are mangled
Into mediocrity
Standardised to fit
An outmoded world
That does not care
About their feelings or their gifts
Or the gifts
Of the very earth itself

A world often interested in using
Controlling, and creating
Obedient fake identities

Where the virtual reality of TV
Games, and smart phones
Offers kids more promise
Than the life
Configured all around them

School children wait
In shelter after shelter
For the bus

I wish for them
A school of a kind
Interested in nourishing
Their innate delight in learning
And kindling the flames
Of their unique spontaneity
Aliveness and creativity
And helping them become
Knowledgeable, mindful, and emotionally aware

That they may discover and gain competence
In the magic of evolving
And the sharing of their gifts
As they come to blossom
And offer up their wisdom
As well as their hearts
To a world in need of both

The idea for this poem came the other morning driving into town along a bus route for a school run. How angry and depressed the faces of so many of the kids waiting for the bus, how dejected were their postures. I found myself thinking why wouldn't they feel depressed if they were heading for an institution of a kind that does not care about them.

Of course school is not always the way I depict it in the first part of the poem. Some schools are wonderful, encouraging, creative, enlivening places that students and teachers alike just love to attend. And yet… for a number school still is not like that.

Every child is different. Each has unique challenges and gifts in need of nourishment and support. Just as every teacher has unique skills and gifts to share. Would that schools were places nourishing and treasuring of pupils and teachers alike. Would that there was space for freedom and diversity.

The Flower That You Are: All You Want To Do

The time may come
When all you want to do
Is be
The flower that you are.

No more pruning or pretending,
Bending out of shape,
Or forcing blossoms
Out of season.
No more trying to be a rose
When finally you know,
You are
A morning glory.

One day you might find
That in the place that suits you
Your heart will open like a blossom
And offer all its beauty
To the sky.

And all you want to do
Is be
In that place,
Surrender to the seasons
And cherish life
As it unfolds.

Yes, the time may come
When all you want to do
Is be
The flower that you are.

"The Flower That You Are" says something about a journey, and a moment, of self-realization. Tradition has it that the morning glory represents love, which is why it was chosen for this poem. Its flowers bloom and die in just one day. However such is the strength and steadfastness of the plant that it constantly creates new flowers. Just like the experiences of love, though they may be steadfast and strong, they are also constantly created anew each time we experience the presence of the beloved or the divine.

So here's to being the flowers that we are, living and being what we love.

Here's to surrendering to life's journey and trusting the wisdom of the heart, and the knowing of the soul as they come to blossom.

Cherry Blossoms: Darkness And Light

The sight of all that pinken effervescence
Right above me brings tears.

I reach for a branch
And run the silken softness of petals
Along my cheek
Wiping the teardrops away.

Then I wander on
Through filigree shadows
Caste on the ground
By the trees.

An interwoven web
Of darkness and light
Rendering
The vulnerable vitality
Of this world.

A day of sunshine yesterday, though the wind was chill. It was a perfect day to wander through the park and see the cherry blossoms that had just come into bloom.

How my heart melted at the sight! I was wreathed in soft smiles and tears as I passed beneath that blushing petal canopy.

Seems I was not the only one out delighting. The park was thronged with people communing with the blossoms, hearts open, cameras clicking, many hugging amidst the flowers, taking selfies, from big burly men to small children. The moment imbued with much tenderness.

The crowd was not unlike those blossoms. Abundant, vulnerable yet vibrant, each unique yet part of a greater whole. I felt touched to be among them. I believed it to be an antidote to all the harsh worrisome experiences and images that can so plague our world. A potent reminder that life and humanity can also be like this.

The Garden Of Your Love: For A Wedding

Into the sweet
celebration of this day,
and the blessing
bestowed by existence
on two hearts
having found one another
and fallen in love,
comes the poem:

When peace and love
are mutually bestowed,
when they are the gifts
you give to yourself,
one another, your family,
your friends, your community,
and the very earth itself,
peace and love will be
the present
that is offered to the world.

And the world is going crazy
for want of presence, peace and love…

So tend the garden of your love
that it may always be a place
where you may flourish.

Remember
the moment one
claims mastery over

the other,
love will be lost.
Remember
you have not come together
to tell one another
who and how to be.

You have come together
to discover and encourage
the mystery and the gift
of who you really are,
and mutually delight
in the synergy
of that unfolding.

You have come together
to mend the places
where the heart has been broken
and love has ceased to flow
that it may grace you once again.

May your connecting be a haven then
of ongoing safety and attraction.
May you cherish this sacred space,
hold it precious,
that your hearts be free to feel
your souls free to be,
and the genuine in you
free to be present.

May you ever blossom
in the garden of your love.

A friend is getting married. I am invited to the wedding. As soon as I heard I felt to write a poem. Something to honour the sacredness of not only the day, but also the gift of two hearts falling in love.

Indeed this is precious. Something to be celebrated and cherished that the special synergy of two hearts beating with love may continue to unfold, and be a blessing for not only the couple but also for all who may encounter them.

Epilogue

Wisdom Awakening: A Poem In Three Parts

Wisdom Awakening One: Being Called Home

Drought in California
Blizzards in New England
Floods in northern Europe
And more.
Much much more.

The very earth,
Like your bodies and your souls,
Is calling out for compassion
And for wisdom
To awaken.

These are difficult days.
The earth and humanity are suffering.
Any personal struggle is a collective struggle too.
Any personal breakthrough
Is a breakthrough for humanity.

These are dark times.
Yet you each have unique
Contributions to be made
Contributions that will also
Bring you joy.

You are called home now.
Home to the earth,
Home to your hearts
And to
Your inner wisdom.

Wisdom Awakening Two: Connecting With Your Soul Child

Returning to your inner wisdom
Means connecting
With the soul child within,
That delicate yet vital vibration,
The essence,
Of who you are.

It means
Honouring what s/he feels,
Soothing any pain,
And cherishing what s/he loves…

S/he is a fount for your wisdom
And a guide for your life.
Your soul child knows
In this you can trust.

So allow yourself to soften
And to let go
Of all the 'shoulds' you have amassed,
All the expectations you keep on repeating
That keep you separate from your child
And the wisdom of existence
As it flows through you.

This means bringing awareness to the wounds
That keep you from your deeper knowing
That you might align with your true work,
Your true friends,
And find your true path and place.

It means gathering with others
In pods of kindliness and love
That you may support one another
And intensify the light.

You need one another for this,
And the world needs
Your light.

Doing what you are called to do,
That which cherishes
The valiant vulnerability and vitality of your soul child,
Cherishes the heart and what it loves,
Means saying no
To all not attuned to your soul's purpose
That you might say yes
To all that is.

This may include doing nothing.
Sometimes a simple surrender
Into being in the moment
Is all that is needed
For wisdom to awaken.

Realising there is nothing you ought to do,
Is a profoundly healing and
Creative act.

Wisdom Awakening Three: A Sacred Union

This is a time calling for integrity,
A reunion of feminine and masculine energies within.

The feminine allows you to hold,
Listen to, receive, and reflect
The knowing of the child,
The wisdom of insight,
And of the divine.

The masculine has the ability to strategize and act
In support of the feminine and the child,
Bringing their intelligence into being,
Such that his actions
Sourced in wholeness,
Are sound.

This calls for a sacred union of all three:
Woman, man, and child.
They need one another
And they need connection
For the heart to flourish.

Creating and inhabiting
Unfolding paths
Of empathy, connectedness, and love,
Is of the essence,
Now.

For the very earth
Like your bodies and your souls
Is crying out
For your delicate vital vibration,
For your return to your heart
And for your wisdom
To awaken.

This poem came in moments of stillness as so many of my poems, do. It seems a good way to complete the book, as in some ways it speaks to essence of the work, and perhaps even to the essence of these times?

Thank you for travelling with me on this journey of awakening and cherishing the heart.

Nanna Aida Svendsen
Stockholm April 2015